MUNICIPAL GOVERNMENT

by Steve Goldsworthy

Weigl

Published by Weigl Educational Publishers Limited
6325 10th Street S.E.
Calgary, AB T2H 2Z9
Website: www.weigl.com

Library and Archives Canada Cataloguing-in-Publication Data available upon request.
Fax (403) 233-7769 WEIGL for the attention of the Publishing Records department.

ISBN 978-1-55388-679-2 (hard cover)
ISBN 978-1-55388-683-9 (soft cover)

Printed in the United States of America in North Mankato, Minnesota
1 2 3 4 5 6 7 8 9 0 14 13 12 11 10

082010
WEP230610

Project Coordinator: Heather C. Hudak
Project Editor: Emily Dolbear
Photo Research: Edward A. Thomas
Design: Tammy West

Weigl acknowledges Getty Images as its primary image supplier for this title.

We gratefully acknowledge the financial support of the Government of Canada
through the Canada Book Fund for our publishing activities.

CONTENTS

Introduction to Canada's Government

Large groups of people need rules for each member to follow. Most countries, cities, and towns have a government for this purpose. Government also organizes large groups of people to accomplish things an individual could not do alone. Most governments, for example, make and enforce laws, collect taxes, construct roads and bridges, educate children, and provide for defence.

Many countries, such as Canada, have a democratic form of government. The words *democratic* and *democracy* come from the Greek words *demos*, or "people," and *kratos*, or "power." In other words, the people have power.

There are two forms of democracy: **direct democracy** and **representative democracy**. Direct democracy gives every citizen the right to vote on every issue.

Athens and many other city-states in ancient Greece governed themselves in this way. Requiring citizens across a large country to gather, debate ideas, and vote on every issue is not practical, however.

Most democratic countries, including Canada, are representative democracies. Citizens elect representatives to attend meetings, vote on issues, and make laws for them. Each person has a voice in government by voting in elections. However, only a small group of representatives has the power to make decisions.

Canada has three levels of government. Each level of government has its own powers and responsibilities. The federal government controls matters common to all provinces and territories. Provincial and territorial governments handle matters that are unique to each province and territory. **Municipal** governments manage matters that affect individual cities, towns, villages, and other municipalities.

Canada's largest municipality is Toronto, Ontario.

Think about it!

1. List three things your government does that you could not do alone.

2. Why do you think Canada is a representative rather than direct democracy?

3. Can you think of some advantages and disadvantages of having a representative government?

What is Municipal Government?

Services such as maintenance of local roads and sewage systems are the job of municipal governments.

Municipal governments are local governments set up by the provincial or territorial legislature to handle local services. Cities, **metropolitan** regions, towns, villages, **counties**, and districts are examples of municipal governments.

Municipal governments have many responsibilities. They often provide police officers and firefighters to protect the community. They build and maintain roads and sidewalks. Cities and towns supply water, waste collection, and recycling services. They might manage public transportation such as buses and trains. Responsibilities can include developing and maintaining parks and other green spaces. Municipal governments often help plan, or zone, industrial and residential areas and issue building permits. They run local health centres, libraries, and educational facilities. Many cities and towns also create and support local arts and cultural programs.

Powers and Responsibilities in Government

This list shows some of the powers and responsibilities that fall under each level of Canada's three levels of government. Some of these responsibilities are shared.

Federal Government

- taxation (direct and indirect)
- national defence
- regulation of trade and commerce
- foreign policy
- criminal law and procedure
- citizenship and immigration
- employment insurance
- money and banking
- patents and copyrights
- census and statistics
- Indian affairs and Northern development
- postal service

Provincial Government

- direct taxation in the province
- civil law
- provincial courts
- natural resources and environment
- hospitals
- provincial prisons
- social services
- education

The territorial governments (Yukon Territory, Northwest Territories, and Nunavut) have many of the same powers as the provinces. Their powers are not guaranteed by the **Constitution**, however.

Municipal Government

- electric utilities
- economic development
- water and sewage
- emergency services
- libraries
- public transit
- land-use planning
- waste collection and recycling
- animal control

The Structure of Municipal Government

F or many years, Canada was a British colony, subject to British rules and laws. Like Canada's federal government, Canadian municipal government is based on the British system of government. The first formal municipality in what is now Canada was Saint John in New Brunswick. It received royal approval from Great Britain in 1785.

The British Parliament passed the Municipal Corporations Act in 1835. This act changed how Great Britain formed, operated, and elected its municipal governments. Some 178 boroughs received permission to set up their own elected town **councils,** headed by a **mayor**.

New Brunswick's Saint John, shown here in a photograph from 1860, became Canada's first formal municipality in 1785.

The Legislative Assembly of the Province of Canada, today's Ontario and Quebec, passed its own version of the Municipal Corporations Act in 1849. This act gave power to local municipal governments to collect taxes and pass local **ordinances** called **by-laws**. They raise most of their **revenue** through taxes on the properties in their municipality. Today, Canada has about 4,000 municipal governments.

In Yellowknife, near the Legislative Assembly of the Northwest Territories building, flags from each of the territories' 33 communities fly. Each flagpole has a plaque with the community's official name and local Aboriginal name.

Intergovernmental Relations

The SkyTrain transit system operates in Vancouver with funding help from the provincial government of British Columbia.

Although municipal government may seem to operate independently, it is closely connected to the country's federal and provincial governments. In Canada, much of a municipal government's power comes from its province or territory. By law, a provincial or territorial government may alter the powers, responsibilities, methods of election, or financial structure of one of its municipalities.

It may even eliminate a municipality altogether. Many local by-laws require provincial or territorial approval. Municipal government budgets also depend on **transfer payments** called **grants** from provincial governments.

Municipal governments share an important relationship with Canada's federal government. The federal government gives them money to construct roads, develop cultural and arts activities, and run social service programs.

Canada's national government also offers assistance to municipal governments in many other ways. Federal departments, such as Transport Canada, help cities and towns build railways, harbours, and airports. The country's housing agency, the Canada Mortgage and Housing Corporation, works with municipal governments on related policy issues. The Royal Canadian Mounted Police, the national policing force, operates in more than 190 municipalities and 184 Aboriginal communities throughout the country.

Large Canadian municipalities, such as Toronto, share some of their operating expenses with provincial and federal governments.

In 1904, King Edward VII gave Canada's federal police force the prefix "Royal" to recognize its service to the country and the Empire.

Royal Canadian Mounted Police officers assist cities and towns in maintaining order.

Types of Municipal Governments

Melissa Blake became mayor of Fort McMurray, Alberta, in 2004. Like most mayors, she presides over city council meetings, among many other duties.

There are different kinds of municipal governments in Canada. Population size helps define what they are called and what they do.

Cities have large populations, many responsibilities, and elected city councils with a mayor to run them. In British Columbia and Saskatchewan, a town can become a city after it reaches a population of 5,000. A municipality in Alberta or Ontario requires 10,000 residents to be called a city.

Towns, villages, parishes, and hamlets are smaller than cities. They also usually elect a council and a mayor. The province of Quebec has no legal distinction between a city and town. It calls each a **ville**.

Some provinces organize areas into counties or regional districts. Often the most important job of governments in these places is maintaining roads. Sparsely populated rural municipalities often cannot afford active local government.

The city of Regina, in Saskatchewan, has more than 150,000 residents.

Change Islands, in Newfoundland and Labrador, was incorporated as a town in 1951. Its population is in the hundreds.

Municipal Councils

A municipal government most often operates with a local council. A municipality's own province or territory sets out rules about council powers, responsibilities, membership, and elections.

The council is made up of elected officials called **councillors**, or sometimes **aldermen**. Cities and towns usually elect councillors to represent a single municipal district, or **ward**. Councils are often made up of between 5 and 20 members. Some cities have larger councils. The number varies with the province or territory as well as the size of the municipality.

The decision-making body of a city or town is called a municipal council.

Gregor Robertson was elected mayor of Vancouver in 2008.

A mayor, sometimes called a **reeve** or a **warden**, leads a council. Most councils carry out legislative and executive tasks. That means they create and enforce by-laws. A council is responsible for the day-to-day operations of its municipality. The support of a **majority** of council members is required for all council decisions, including passing by-laws.

Local Leaders

A mayor is the chairperson of a city or town council. A reeve is the president of the council in rural municipalities and in some villages in central and western Canada. A warden is the head of a county council in Quebec and the Maritime Provinces. Mayor, reeve, and warden are usually elected positions.

The Power of By-laws

Citizens may organize demonstrations to show support or opposition to particular by-laws.

One of the most important functions of any municipal council is enacting and enforcing by-laws. These are public ordinances that apply to a specific municipality. According to Canadian law, local councils or municipal governments get their powers from another governing body, such as a provincial or the federal government. As a result, local by-laws cannot contradict existing provincial or federal laws.

The town or city council votes on by-laws. Councillors usually propose by-laws or changes to by-laws during council meetings. Citizens may even recommend by-laws to their councillor.

By-laws may be related to vehicle parking, use of parks and other recreation areas, noise control, building and construction safety, or zoning and business regulation.

Enforcement of these by-laws is also the responsibility of municipal government. The council appoints by-law enforcement officers to monitor and police citizens. Those who do not follow the rules outlined in by-laws may be charged with a criminal offence or be subject to a fine.

Some Interesting By-laws

- Homeowners must clear their sidewalks within 24 hours of a snowfall. *Kitchener, Ontario*

- The total number of cats and dogs in a residence cannot exceed five. *Ottawa, Ontario*

- No one can make noise that disturbs the peace in a public place. *Vancouver, British Columbia*

- Tree climbing is not permitted. *Oshawa, Ontario*

- When washing your car on your private property, you must use only water and no soap. *Calgary, Alberta*

Key People in Municipal Government

I t takes many elected officials and employees to run a municipal government. Here are some of the key people and groups.

Mayor

A mayor is elected by the town or city citizens. He or she is head of the local government. Mayors attend council meetings and sit on committees. Meetings are held during regular business hours and in the evenings. A mayor's job includes representing the municipality at official events.

David Miller was first elected mayor of Toronto in 2003.

Councillor

A councillor, sometimes called an alderman, is elected by the voters in a municipality or in a ward. He or she may belong to, but does not represent, a **political party**. The job of a councillor is to represent community members at the council. Councillors attend meetings and sit on a range of committees and boards, such as a library board or a community safety committee.

Shelley Carroll became a city councillor for Toronto's Ward 33 in 2003.

Council

A council sets up, manages, and budgets for community services. A council also proposes and votes on by-laws. Sometimes, it forms task groups to address specific concerns, such as land-use planning or youth unemployment. A council must draw up a yearly budget for its activities. It raises money from local property taxes, various public service fees, fines, and grants from the federal and provincial governments.

The city council of Montreal meets once a month.

City Manager

Large cities use a chief administrative officer, or **city manager**, to administer all municipal departments and their employees. The city manager's office is responsible for carrying out the city council's policies.

Boards and Commissions

Many municipal governments have independent boards and commissions, with elected members. Police commissions oversee local police forces. School boards meet regularly to make curriculum, salary, and busing decisions. Other boards address issues related to health, parks and recreation, and public transit.

Department and Staff Workers

Most municipal governments have departments and various offices. City and town departments include public works, finance, and human resources. In villages or small towns, one person may serve as municipal clerk, tax collector, and by-law officer. In large cities, these responsibilities might require hundreds of workers.

City Hall: The Calgary Model

A clock tower crowns the historic city hall in Calgary. The clock, which workers wind every week, has kept near perfect time since its installation in 1910.

Municipal governments operate in many kinds of buildings. They include simple portable buildings in rural areas, country town halls, historic city halls, and modern towers. Municipal government buildings are as diverse as the communities they serve.

The city hall in Calgary represents a typical big-city structure. The heart of this municipal government, like most municipalities, is the city council. The council has one mayor who represents the entire city and 14 councillors, or aldermen, who represent single wards. These officials serve three-year terms.

Calgary's city council relies on its four policy committees, composed of aldermen, to help run the city. These committees recommend policies on operations and environment, finance, transportation, and community services. The four policy committees gather at city hall once a month for a public meeting. Many aldermen also sit on special committees, boards, and authorities that address issues such as parking, civic planning, and preservation of heritage sites.

The city council meets three Mondays a month in council chambers at city hall. The first two meetings of the month are to discuss suggestions from the four policy committees.

The last meeting of the month is a public hearing where citizens give their opinions.

The city manager's office is responsible for carrying out the city council's policies. The city manager leads the office and an executive team to oversee the planning and operation of the city administration.

The multi-tiered Calgary Municipal Building and City Hall opened in 1985.

Toronto's City Council

The city council of Toronto, Canada's largest city, operates like many other cities in Canada. City council members serve on policy and executive committees. Each committee reports to the council.

City Council

Executive Committees

Standing Policy Committees

Executive
- Budget
- Employee & Labour Relations
- Affordable Housing

Committees report to Executive Committee

Community Development & Recreation

Economic Development

Public Works & Infrastructure

Government Management

Parks & Environment

Planning & Growth Management

Licensing & Standards

Committees report to Council. Chairs sit on Executive Committee

The Election Process

Voters must show proof of their identity and address at their polling station.

Whether running for mayor of a large city or councillor in a small village, a candidate must be at least 18 years of age and a citizen of Canada. In most cases, a candidate must have been a resident of his or her province or territory for at least six months. Some municipalities require candidates to be nominated by at least two people. They may have to pay a small nomination deposit, which is usually $100. Candidates may collect contributions to fund their campaigns.

In small communities, citizens have the right to vote for all of the members of council. Larger cities are divided into wards. Each ward elects its own councillor. Voters choose their mayor in a separate election from the council election. A mayor or councillor serves a term of three to four years, depending on the province or territory.

At the federal and provincial level, candidates run as members of political parties. At the municipal level, however, there are usually no political parties. Only Vancouver and Montreal have ever had municipal candidates with party affiliations.

A voter must be at least 18 years of age and a citizen of Canada. In most areas, a voter must also have been a resident of his or her province or territory for at least six months and have lived in the municipality for at least 30 days.

Voting in elections at all levels is part of the political process.

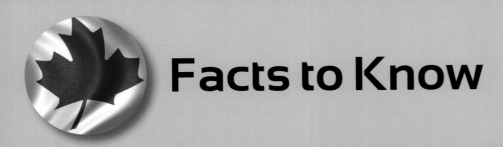

Facts to Know

Municipal Revenue in Canada

Cities, towns, and villages receive revenue from property taxes paid by local homeowners, other taxes, permits and licenses, public service fees, and fines. All of this money is called own-source revenue. The remaining municipal revenue comes from transfer payments from the federal and provincial governments. The following chart shows the revenue received by all of Canada's local general governments in 2008.

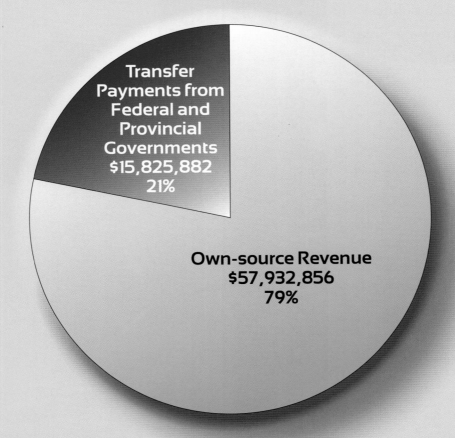

Transfer Payments from Federal and Provincial Governments
$15,825,882
21%

Own-source Revenue
$57,932,856
79%

TOTAL REVENUE: $73,758,738
All dollar values are in thousands.

Canada's Major Cities and Their Populations

Four out of five Canadians live in large, metropolitan areas. Here are the populations of some of Canada's cities.

City Populations

1. Vancouver, British Columbia – 578,000 (metropolitan area 2.1 million)
2. Calgary, Alberta – 1.07 million
3. Regina, Saskatchewan – 179,246
4. Winnipeg, Manitoba – 675,100
5. Toronto, Ontario – 2.5 million (metropolitan area 5.5 million)
6. Ottawa, Ontario – 812,135
7. Montreal, Quebec – 1.6 million
8. Quebec City, Quebec – 491,140
9. Moncton, New Brunswick – 124,055
10. Halifax, Nova Scotia – 372,679
11. Charlottetown, Prince Edward Island – 32,174
12. St. John's, Newfoundland and Labrador – metropolitan area 181,113
13. Whitehorse, Yukon Territory – 25,690
14. Yellowknife, Northwest Territories – 18,700
15. Iqaluit, Nunavut – 6,184

Toronto and Its Wards

When Toronto was incorporated as a city in 1834, it had a mayor and a city council elected by wards. The council chose a mayor from its ranks.

Today, voters in Toronto elect their mayor directly. With the mayor, the city council has 45 members. Each councillor represents a ward. The map below shows Toronto's 44 wards.

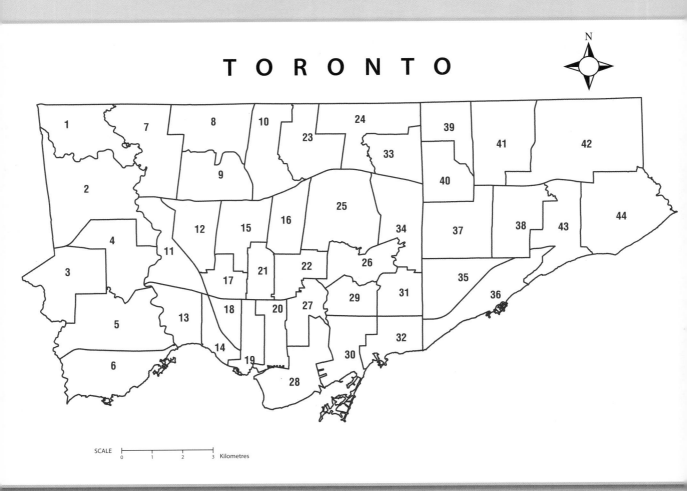

T O R O N T O

N

SCALE
0   1   2   3   Kilometres

How Toronto Allocates Its Money

In 2009, the city of Toronto had a budget of $8.7 billion. This pie chart shows how the city government allocated the money.

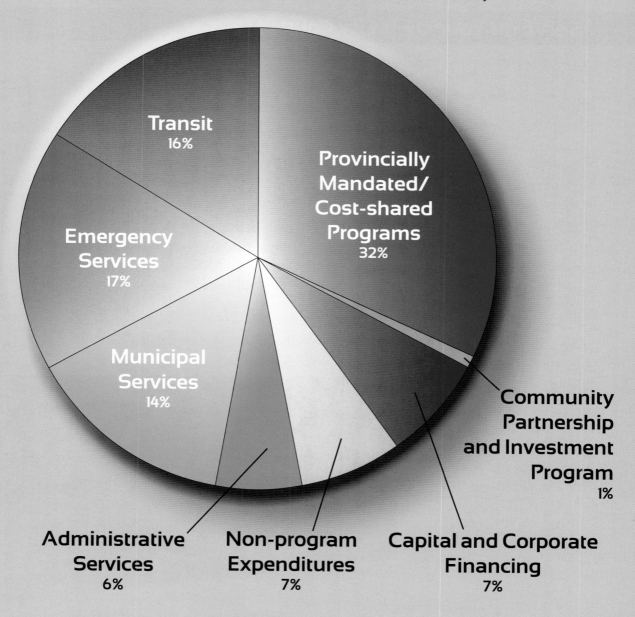

- Transit 16%
- Provincially Mandated/Cost-shared Programs 32%
- Emergency Services 17%
- Municipal Services 14%
- Administrative Services 6%
- Non-program Expenditures 7%
- Capital and Corporate Financing 7%
- Community Partnership and Investment Program 1%

Provincially Mandated/Cost-shared Programs

- Affordable Housing Office
- Children's Services
- Court Services
- Long-term Care Homes and Services
- Shelter, Support, and Housing Administration
- Social Development, Finance, and Administration
- Toronto Employment and Social Services
- Toronto Public Health

Activities

Serve on Your Own City Council

Now that you have learned about municipal government, try organizing a city council in your classroom or with friends.

Each person is a council member representing a single ward. Name your wards after local neighbourhoods, or make up your own names. Decide on one person to serve as the mayor.

It is now time to set up committees. Pick a few interesting issues, such as pet ownership, parks and playground planning, or ways to promote healthful living. Each committee must do research on its topic before the "council" holds its own public city council meeting.

The mayor calls the meeting to order. Each committee presents problems and solutions in its area of concern.

Debate each issue. Ask questions and listen carefully to the answers.

When you have discussed each topic, take a vote on what actions to take. An action must win a majority of votes to be approved. Keep in mind that you must serve the greater good of all of your citizens to make your city the best it can be.

How did the activity go? Were you able to persuade other councillors to change their minds? Did anyone change your mind? Have a discussion about what skills might be most valuable in a city councillor.

Become a City Council Reporter

Reporters help inform the public about the issues and activities of local government. Try your hand at being a junior city council reporter.

Plan a field trip to your city or town hall to attend a council meeting.

On the day of your visit, conduct yourself like a member of the press. A reporter's greatest tool is his or her ability to observe. Watch and listen to everything. Take notes. Are any by-laws being proposed? What are the issues at stake? How might they impact you or your neighbours? Do you think the issues discussed are important? Why?

In advance, try to set up an interview with a city councillor for after the meeting. Prepare your questions in advance. Ask questions that begin with *Who*, *What*, *Where*, *When*, and *How*. "Who proposed the new by-law?" "When will the proposed new bridge be built?" "Why does the new recycling program cost so much?" Write down the answers, and use them to write a news story.

WHAT Have You LEARNED?

Answer these questions to see what you have learned about Canada's municipal government.

1 What does municipal government do?

2 Who has ultimate power over a municipality?

3 Which city became Canada's first municipality in 1785?

4 What is the name of the most common type of head of municipal government?

5 What is the most common name for a municipal district represented by a councillor?

6 What is a municipal law called?

7 What is a city manager?

8 How many members does the Calgary city council have?

9 Name the two requirements to run for municipal office.

10 What Canadian city has the largest population?

ANSWERS: 1. *Municipal government handles local services for a city, metropolitan region, town, village, county, or district.* 2. *Its province or territory* 3. *Saint John, New Brunswick* 4. *A mayor* 5. *A ward* 6. *A by-law* 7. *A city manager is the chief administrative officer of a municipality.* 8. *15 (one mayor and 14 aldermen)* 9. *All candidates must be at least 18 years of age and citizens of Canada.* 10. *Toronto, Ontario, with 2.5 million people (metropolitan area, 5.5 million)*

Find Out More

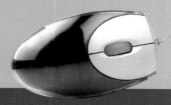

Many books and websites provide information on municipal government. To learn more about municipal government, borrow books from the library or do research online.

BOOKS

Most libraries have computers with an online catalog. If you input a key word, you will get a list of related books in the library. Nonfiction books are arranged numerically by call number. Fiction books are organized alphabetically by the author's last name.

WEBSITES

Libraries often have online reference databases that you can access from any computer. You can also use an Internet search engine, but be sure to verify the source of the website's information. Official websites run by government agencies are usually reliable, for example. To find out more about municipal governments, type key words, such as "Canada's system of municipal government," "Canada's cities, towns, and villages," or the name of a Canadian municipality, into the search field.

Words to Know

aldermen: councillors

by-laws: local ordinances; municipal laws

city manager: the chief administrative officer who manages all municipal departments and their employees

constitution: the fundamental principles and rules under which a country is governed

councillors: elected members of a municipal council

councils: legislative groups for cities or towns

counties: divisions of a province that may have their own municipal governments

direct democracy: a form of government that gives every citizen the right to vote on every issue

grants: transfers of money, such as from one level of government to another

majority: more than half of a total

mayor: the head of a city or town council

metropolitan: relating to a region including a city and the densely populated surrounding areas

municipal: related to small territories governed by elected officials, such as cities, towns, or villages

ordinances: local laws or regulations enacted by a municipal council

political party: a group of people who share similar ideas about how government should operate

reeve: the president of the council in rural municipalities and in some villages in central and western Canada

representative democracy: a form of government in which citizens do not take part directly but elect representatives to pass laws and make decisions on behalf of everyone

revenue: money received, such as money collected by a government through taxes

transfer payments: direct payments from governments to other governments or to individuals

ville: a city or a town in Quebec

ward: a municipal district represented by a councillor

warden: the head of a county council in Quebec and the Maritime Provinces

INDEX